LIFE ON A
VIKING SHIP

JANE SHUTER

www.heinemann.co.uk/library

Visit our website to find out more information about Heinemann Library books.

To order:

 Phone 44 (0) 1865 888066

 Send a fax to 44 (0) 1865 314091

💻 Visit the Heinemann Bookshop at www.heinemann.co.uk/library to browse our catalogue and order online.

First published in Great Britain by Heinemann Library, Halley Court, Jordan Hill, Oxford OX2 8EJ, part of Harcourt Education.
Heinemann is a registered trademark of Harcourt Education Ltd.

© Harcourt Education Ltd 2005
First published in paperback in 2006
The moral right of the proprietor has been asserted.

Editors: Nancy Dickmann and
  Sarah Chappelow
Design: Ron Kamen and
  Dave Oakley/Arnos Design
Illustrations: Barry Atkinson
Maps: Jeff Edwards
Picture Researcher: Erica Newbery
  and Elaine Willis
Production Controller: Camilla Smith

Originated by Modern Age
Printed and bound in China
by WKT Company Limited

10 dig ISBN 0 431 04298 5 (hardback)
13 dig ISBN 978 0431 042985
09 08 07 06 05
10 9 8 7 6 5 4 3 2 1

10 dig ISBN 0 431 04303 5 (paperback)
13 dig ISBN 978 0431 04305 6
10 09 08 07 06
10 9 8 7 6 5 4 3 2 1

British Library Cataloguing in Publication Data
Shuter, Jane
Life on a Viking ship. - (Picture the past)
387.5'0948'09021
A full catalogue record for this book is available from the British Library.

Acknowledgements:
The publishers would like to thank the following for permission to reproduce photographs: AAAC p. **26**; AKG pp. **16**, **20** (Jurgen Sorges); Bridgeman p. **12**; Corbis pp. **9** (Ted Spiegal), **15** (Ted Spiegal), **22**; National Museum of Denmark p. **11**; Werner Forman pp. **7**, **8**, **10**, **18**, **19**; York Archaeological Trust pp. **6**, **14**, **24**, **27**.

Cover photograph of a stone carving of a Viking ship reproduced with permission of AKG.

Every effort has been made to contact copyright holders of any material reproduced in this book. Any omissions will be rectified in subsequent printings if notice is given to the publishers.

Contents

Any words appearing in bold, **like this**, are explained in the Glossary.

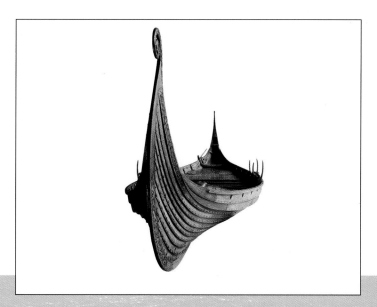

Who were the Vikings?

The Vikings lived in Norway, Sweden and Denmark more than 1,000 years ago. There were lots of different groups of Vikings, all with their own leaders. Ships were important to the Vikings for exploring, **trading**, and fighting. Without their shipbuilding and sailing skills, they could not have spread as widely as they did. They built all their ships in the same way, but had different shapes depending on what they were used for.

Look for these:
The longship shows you the subject of each chapter. The picture of a helmet shows you boxes with interesting facts, figures, and quotes about life on a Viking ship.

TIMELINE OF EVENTS IN THIS BOOK

AD 700 Vikings spread across Norway, Denmark, and Sweden

AD 780 First Viking raids on England

AD 795 First Viking raids on Ireland

AD 799 First Viking raids on France

VIKINGS MOVE ACROSS EUROPE, SAILING UP MAJOR RIVERS AD 800–850

AD 800

As the numbers of Vikings grew, they had to look for new places to farm and settle. They explored by land and by sea.

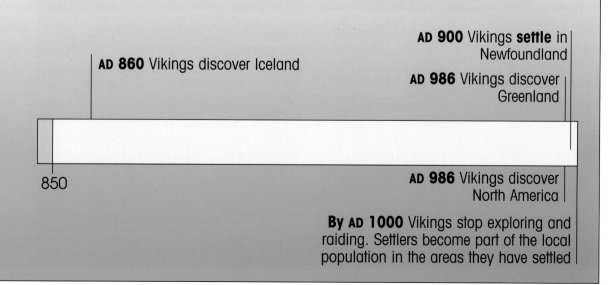

AD **860** Vikings discover Iceland

AD **900** Vikings **settle** in Newfoundland

AD **986** Vikings discover Greenland

850

AD **986** Vikings discover North America

By AD **1000** Vikings stop exploring and raiding. Settlers become part of the local population in the areas they have settled

Building ships

Viking shipmakers made their ships by hand. They shaped the **keel** first – the long, thick piece of wood that ran along the bottom and middle of the ship. Then they added the **end posts** that came up from the keel. They used overlapping planks to make the outside frame. Then they filled the gaps between the planks with a sticky, waterproof liquid called **pitch**.

WOOD

The keel and the end posts of Viking ships were always made from oak. This is because oak is a strong wood. They used oak for the rest of the ship if they had enough. If not, they used other woods such as ash, elm, pine, or larch.

Viking shipbuilders used simple tools, like these. They split wood planks apart by banging wooden wedges into them with the ends of their axes.

Once the outside was finished, the shipbuilders put in the inside **ribs** that ran across the ship to strengthen it. Then they made a block of wood to hold the **mast**. Boards were put across the ribs to make it easier to move around. The boards were lifted to **bail** water out of the ship. This needed doing almost all the time in bad weather, because the ships had low sides.

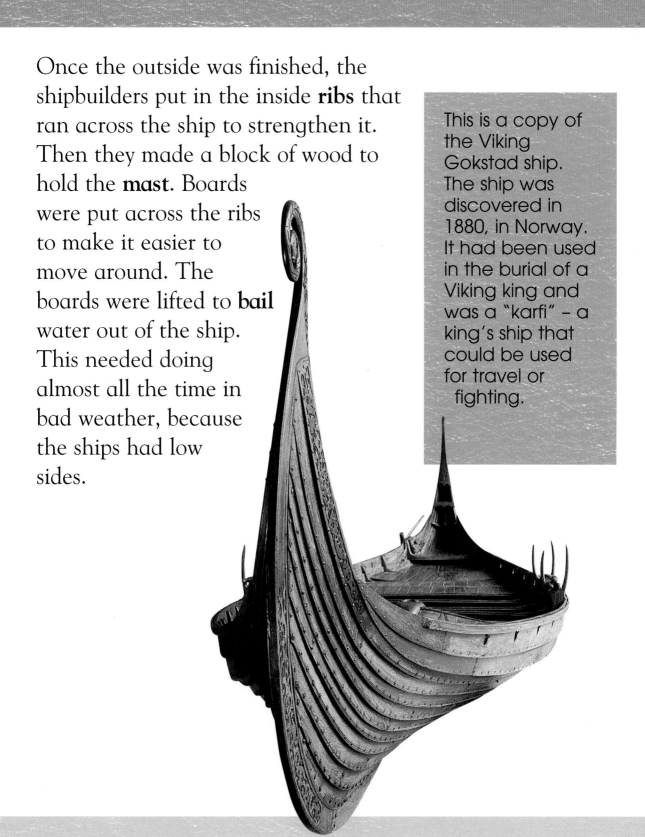

This is a copy of the Viking Gokstad ship. The ship was discovered in 1880, in Norway. It had been used in the burial of a Viking king and was a "karfi" – a king's ship that could be used for travel or fighting.

Once the basic shape of the ship was made, Viking shipbuilders had to add a **mast**, sails, and a **rudder** to steer the ship. The mast fixed into a big wooden block in the middle of the ship and held up the single sail. The sail was big and almost square. It was moved up and down using ropes and weights. The rudder was like a big **oar**, fixed to the back of the right side of the ship.

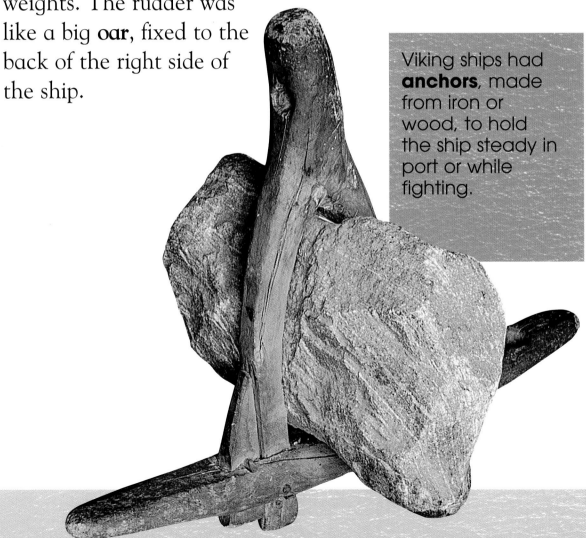

Viking ships had **anchors**, made from iron or wood, to hold the ship steady in port or while fighting.

The ship also needed oars, to use when there was no wind, or when the sail was taken down during fighting. Viking sailors also needed to take supplies to repair the ship – spare cloth, thread, rope, and tools. These were stored in the chests that the Vikings sat on to row the ship.

BRIGHT SAILS

Sails were made of wool or linen. Viking **sagas** say they had checks or blue, red, green, or white stripes. This may have been to help people tell who they were from a distance. Pieces of a sail with red stripes were found in the Gokstad ship.

This carving shows a Viking ship with its sail up. The lines across the sail may have been strips of leather or rope, used to keep the sail's shape.

9

The Vikings used their sails as often as possible. If they had to sail in the direction the wind was coming from the sail did not work, so they rowed the ship. If they did not have enough people to row, they would then sail in a zigzag path. This way they used the wind one way, then the other. But it took a long time.

The Vikings used weathervanes like this brass one to work out which direction the wind was coming from.

The Vikings used to **navigate** by keeping close to the coast and remembering **landmarks**. If they were out of sight of land, they had to rely on the sun or the stars. They invented the pelorus – a compass that let them navigate using the shadows made by the sun. But when the weather was cloudy for a long time, they could get lost.

The Vikings rarely sailed at sea during the winter. A Viking book of advice on sailing, written in 1230, said, "Only set out at the best time. Always have good equipment on your ship. Never stay out at sea too late in the autumn if you can avoid it."

This is part of a pelorus. The whole thing would have been in the shape of a circle.

Warships

Viking **warships** were long and narrow. They floated very well on the water. Their masts could be taken down. All this was so they could sail up rivers, as well as at sea. The Vikings were well known for making surprise attacks on towns and villages by sailing up rivers that bigger boats could not use.

Some warships had carved animal heads like this that could be slotted into the **end posts** of the ship to frighten the enemy.

The Vikings measured warships by how many **oars** the ship had. An average size was 28 oars which needed at least 28 rowers on board. A ship like this was about 17 metres (55 feet) long and 2.5 metres (8 feet) wide. The biggest warship that we know about had 60 oars and the smallest had 24.

The Viking shields fixed on to a piece of wood that ran along the side of the ship. When the Vikings landed, they just lifted them off.

Viking battles

The Vikings did not like to fight out at sea. They liked to fight close to land, in calm water. Before a battle, they put their ships' **masts** down and tied several ships together. This made them less likely to roll over during the fighting. The biggest ship, the king's ship, was in the middle. Some ships were left free, to sail behind the enemy's ships.

The Vikings usually wore very plain, thick helmets. They were shaped to protect their faces and necks in battle.

The battle began with the warriors firing arrows and throwing stones and spears at the enemy ships. They wanted to cause as much damage as they could before getting close. Once the enemy ships were close enough, the Vikings boarded them and fought hand-to-hand, with swords, spears, and axes.

This carving, found on the Island of Lindisfarne, is said to show Viking warriors with swords and axes.

15

Trading ships

Trading ships were designed to carry cargo. The hold, used for storing goods, was 2 metres (6.5 feet) deep. Warships had a hold about 1 metre (3.2 feet) deep. Most trading ships were sailed by five or six people. Often these people were 'sharers'. They bought the boat and the goods together, sailed and traded and then shared out the money they made.

HOW BIG?

Trading ships came in many sizes, but were smaller than warships. An average size was 15 metres (50 feet) long and 4.5 metres (15 feet) wide. It would have had about 12 **oars**, although they were seldom used. A ship this size could carry about 20 tonnes of cargo.

This trading ship was found by underwater archaeologists. They put it back together and repaired it, so we can see what it looked like.

Trading ships often towed smaller boats with them. These could take things further up river.

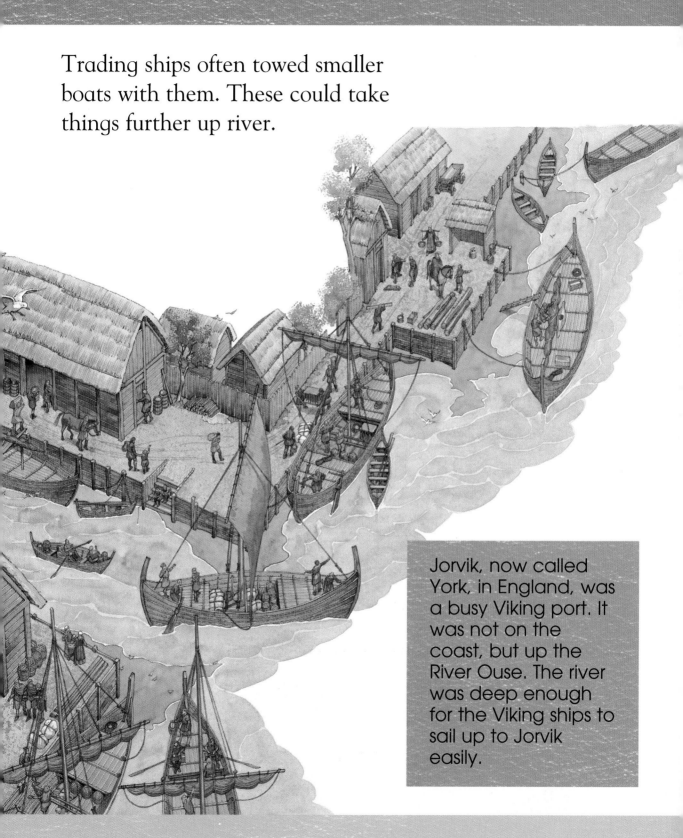

Jorvik, now called York, in England, was a busy Viking port. It was not on the coast, but up the River Ouse. The river was deep enough for the Viking ships to sail up to Jorvik easily.

Trade

We know that the Vikings used to **trade** widely, because **goods** from many parts of the world have been found in Viking graves. They traded through the Mediterranean Sea and up long, wide European rivers like the Volga.

This statue of Buddha, from India, was found in a Swedish grave. It shows just how far Viking traders travelled.

A KING'S FEAST?

The Viking king who was buried in the Gokstad ship (see page 7) was buried with many possessions. These included horses, dogs, and a peacock, which must have come from around India. We do not know if the peacock was buried as an expensive pet or an expensive meal!

The Vikings traded fur, fat, fish, and **slaves** for wine, silk, and spices. Traders often carried their own scales and weights, to make sure they were not cheated. They traded the goods they bought at trading towns around the Viking world, such as Jorvik or Hedeby.

These coins, found in Sweden, came from many places in the Viking world. They include Arabic coins – the Arabs traded widely too.

Explorers' ships

The Vikings went exploring in ships that were more like **cargo** ships in shape, with deep holds, but which had more **oars**. It was the Viking men who went exploring. Sometimes, several ships went together, led by the king. They explored by working their way along from one island or piece of mainland to another.

This is a modern copy of Viking homes at Vinland. The builders used the same tools and ways of building as the Vikings did.

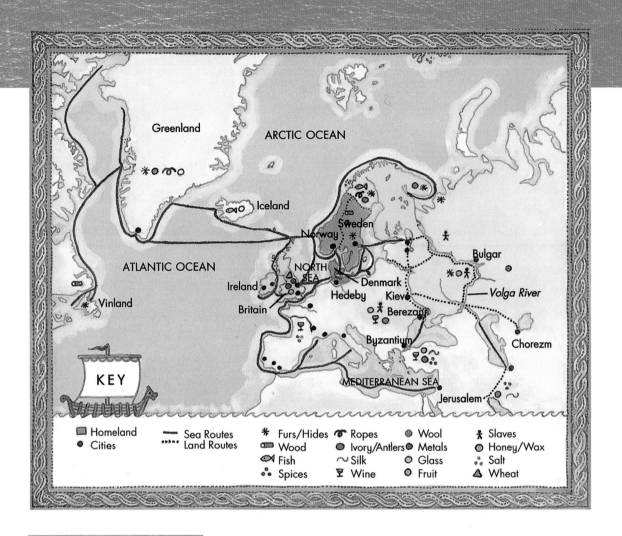

The map shows the following locations and labels:

- Greenland
- ARCTIC OCEAN
- Iceland
- Sweden
- Norway
- ATLANTIC OCEAN
- NORTH SEA
- Ireland
- Denmark
- Hedeby
- Britain
- Kiev
- Berezan
- Bulgar
- Volga River
- Chorezm
- Vinland
- Byzantium
- MEDITERRANEAN SEA
- Jerusalem

KEY

▢ Homeland	✳ Furs/Hides	☁ Ropes	⦿ Wool	⚱ Slaves
● Cities	⬭ Wood	◉ Ivory/Antlers	◉ Metals	◉ Honey/Wax
― Sea Routes	◁ Fish	∼ Silk	◯ Glass	⸪ Salt
⋯ Land Routes	⋰ Spices	⚱ Wine	◉ Fruit	△ Wheat

The Vikings explored to **trade** in new places, and then often settled in places they had started trading in. This map shows how far the Vikings went.

The Vikings carried spare cloth with them, for mending the sail. They also carried a wooden tent frame. They used the sail and the tent frame to make a covered area to eat and sleep in when they were not actually sailing. If they were close to land, they camped on the beach.

The homeland of the Vikings, Denmark, Norway, and Sweden, did not have much good farmland. Growing numbers of Vikings meant they needed to explore to find new places to live. Explorers preferred to find land where there were few or no other people. But the Vikings fought for land if they had to.

FIRST SIGHTINGS

First descriptions of a new land almost always described how good it looked to **settle** on. So explorers said of Greenland (which was occupied), "the pasture is good, there are large, fine farms there." Explorers to North America said that there were plenty of salmon in the rivers and lakes, "bigger than they had ever seen."

The climate in the Viking homelands was cold. A great deal of land was too steep to farm on.

The Vikings found North America by accident. A merchant called Bjarni Herjolfsson sailed to Greenland in the year 985. He was blown off course and into fog. They finally found land, but it was too flat to be Greenland. Bjarni refused to go ashore and explore – he headed back for Greenland. As soon as he told what he had seen, others set off to find it.

When Vikings came to a place that was already lived in, they had to fight or make friends with the people living there. This was true even of other Viking groups

Settlers' ships

Settlers travelled in different ways, depending on how many of them were travelling and where they were going. Large groups used ships, like explorers. Sometimes, just a few people wanted to **settle** in a place where Vikings already lived. Then, they could travel on a **trading** ship going that way.

FITTING IN

Viking settlers sometimes lived just with other Vikings – as at Jorvik, which was a Viking town. But they often settled on farmland, not in a town, among the local people. Then they often began to dress and live like these people.

This Viking mould was used to make Christian crosses and tiny hammers, the symbol of the Viking god Thor. Some Viking settlers became Christian as part of settling in – others did not. So their blacksmiths made symbols for both religions.

The first thing Viking settlers did was build shelters for the animals they had brought and a shelter for their boat. Then they built houses for themselves. They lived in tents while they did this. Depending on the time of year, they began farming while the house was unfinished.

Viking settlers who came to a new place also brought animals, such as pigs and chickens, with them.

Vikings homes had an outside toilet. They had a well that provided water for washing clothes and people. But how did the Vikings wash and go to the toilet while they were at sea? On short trips, they probably skipped washing altogether, especially in cold weather. On longer trips, or in hotter parts of the Viking world, they had to wash in seawater.

Buckets, like this one, were useful on board ship for holding water to wash in. People who did not want to hang over the side of the ship probably also used them as toilets!

We do not know for certain about toilets, but it seems most likely that the Vikings used a bucket, or went directly over the side of the ship. The bucket was probably kept at the back of the ship. It was emptied into the sea and cleaned with seawater every time it was used.

A DIFFERENT VIEW

The Arab traveller, Ibn Fadlan, wrote a description of Vikings living along the Volga River in the year 921. This is how he described their daily washing: "They wash their faces and hands each morning. A girl brings a basin of water to her master and he washes his hands, face, and hair. Then he combs his hair out with a comb in the water. Then he blows his nose and spits into the basin."

Viking women and some men and children had long hair. The men mostly wore beards. They kept their hair and beards clean and tidy by using very fine-toothed combs, which also caught any nits.

Food and drink

The Vikings usually ate two meals a day – breakfast at sunrise and dinner in the evening when the sun set. They ate a lot of meat and even more fish, which they smoked, dried, salted, pickled and ate fresh.

Vikings often had big feasts when they came home from sailing. The men ate, drank, and told stories. The women served the food and ate by themselves, later.

Flatbread

When they were sailing, the Vikings probably took little more than some flatbread and dried fish with them. If the bread got hard on long trips, they soaked it in seawater to soften it.

WARNING: do not cook anything unless there is an adult to help you.

You will need:
3.5 cups of wholemeal bread flour
1.5 cups of skimmed milk
1 egg
a pinch of salt
some toasted stinging nettle leaves (the Vikings did not always add these, but they added some flavour)

1 Heat the oven to 180°C (350°F).

2 Put the flour into a mixing bowl, make a hollow in the centre of the flour and add the egg and half of the milk. Stir with your hands until all the milk has soaked into the flour.

3 Gradually add more of the milk, mixing with your hands as you go until it holds together in one big ball, but is not sticky (if it gets sticky, add more flour).

4 Knead the mixture, pressing and folding it over and over with your hands for at least 4 minutes.

5 Break up into pieces the size of a ping-pong ball. Press these pieces flat.

6 Bake in the oven, on a tray or on the oven rack, for about 10 minutes, until it makes a hollow sound when you tap it.

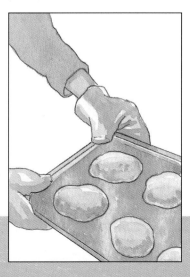

Glossary

anchor heavy object lowered from a ship to the bottom of the sea or river. It has ends that will dig into the bottom to hold the ship in one place.

bail to scoop water out of a ship

birch kind of tree

cargo goods that are taken from one place to another

end posts pieces of wood at each end of the ship that come up from the bottom and which the ship's sides are fixed to

goods things that are bought and sold

keel long, thick piece of wood that runs along the bottom of a ship in the middle

landmarks things on land which are easy to see, and used to navigate by. A landmark might be a funny shaped cliff, clump of trees, hill, or village.

mast wooden pole that sails are hung on

navigate to work out how to get from one place to another

oars shaped pieces of wood used to pull ships through the water

pitch mixture made from the roots of a birch tree, used to make wooden ships waterproof

plane tool used for smoothing and shaping wood

ribs pieces of wood that go across a ship to strengthen it, in the same way that our ribs go across our chests

rudder shaped piece of wood fixed to the end of a ship, which is used to steer

saga Viking adventure story

settle move from one place to live in another

slave person who is bought and sold by someone and has to work for them

trade this can mean: 1 a job

2 selling or swapping goods

warship ship especially used for fighting

Further resources

Books

Explore History: Romans, Anglo-Saxons & Vikings in Britain (Heinemann Library, 2001)

The Saxons and the Vikings (Heinemann Library, 1994)

The Viking World, Christine Hatt (Heinemann Library, 2004)

What happened here?: Viking Street, Marilyn Tolhurst (A & C Black ,1994)

Websites

www.jorvik-viking-centre.co.uk/jorvik-navigation.htm
Use this website to find out all about the Vikings and visit the Jorvik Viking Centre online.

www.pbs.org/wgbh/nova/vikings/
An exciting website that contains video clips to bring the Vikings to life!

www.bbc.co.uk/history/ancient/vikings/
A website packed with information, activities, and animations about the Vikings

www.mnh.si.edu/vikings/start.html
Go on a Viking voyage and learn all about their sagas on this website.

Contacts

Jorvik Viking Centre
Coppergate, York, YO1 9WT

Email: jorvik@yorkarchaeology.co.uk
Tel: 01904 643211

Index